The Albanian National Question and the Myth of Greater Albania

In outlining the frontiers of Albania it has been often necessary to disregard ethnography for larger reasons; but there is no reason to disregard it unnecessarily.

— Robert Vansittart, British Foreign Office[1]

In the late 19th Century Western geographers "condemned" South Eastern Europe, known as Ottoman Europe, by calling it Balkans, which had a negative connotation as Europe's backyard. In addition this reference was racist as it depicted the people who lived there as backward, prone to hatred, and emotionally unstable.[2] Furthermore, they invented the term "Balkanization" that was, according to political scientist James Der Derian, generally acknowledged as "…the break-up of larger political units into smaller, mutually hostile states."[3]

However, what is often forgotten, intentionally or by sheer ignorance, from those who proclaim themselves specialists of the area, is that this region's explosive nature has been largely a product of the interplay of the Great Powers'[4] rivalry. The demise of the Ottoman Empire and newfound interest from the European Great Powers for the "oppressed" not only helped the creation of the new states but also cultivated a degree of animosity between the various ethnic groups that was not seen before. By backing irredentist claims of nationalist leaders described on 'Platforms' or 'Great Ideas' often based upon selective references and interpretations of history, the West sowed the seeds of antagonism and legitimized what is commonly known at present time as 'ethnic cleansing'.

Albanians, as one of the oldest people in the region, have been particularly punished, especially during the late 19th century and 20th century. Their history is characterized by the Great Powers unjust decisions imposed upon them and wars of national survival. Their space has been the object of neighboring countries irredentism, claimed in the south by Greece, to the east by Bulgaria, on the coast by Italy and in the north by Serbia.

After the collapse of the Ottoman Empire the entire Albanian National Question (ANQ) was barely understood by those who had been assigned the responsibility of the determining Albania's fate.[5] Thus, on the first occasion that the governments of the Great Powers confronted the question of a distinct Albanian ethnicity, and after they actively had promoted the claims of Slav-Christian national groups, defined according to current ethnographic criteria, they specifically declined to recognize an equivalent Albanian ethnicity. [6] The creation of Albania was about making a new balance in the Balkans and the geo-political factors were clearly more important than the proclaimed ethnic rationale. "If a good settlement of Albania would mean war between two or more powers, and an inferior settlement would secure peace between them, the latter has to be preferred" Lord Grey declared in February 1913.[7] Diplomats representing the Great Powers, many of whom were wholly ignorant of Balkan affairs, sealed the future of the Albanian nation when they decided to partition it [8] and thus shattered its social, political, and economic cohesion.

There is no similar nation in Europe that lives divided in five different countries like the Albanians.[9] In the late 20th Century, Albanians living outside the Republic of Albania boundaries, in the Balkans and elsewhere, were usually always seen as part of the normal Balkan Diaspora rather than organic parts of a wider nation by the West. Albanians were considered as an unimportant factor in international relations or even in regional Balkan politics. This view prejudiced any serious consideration of their wider political and economic position.[10] The West continually ignored the pleas from more than 2.5 million Albanians living outside Albania's borders In the name of preserving international relations and inviolability of existing boundaries.

However, the ANQ did arrive on the international stage, long after the London Ambassadors Conference in 1913, when Kosova in 1998 and Macedonia in 2001 erupted into conflict and raised the status of the ANQ as a key topic of concern for the International Community (IC). The consequences of these events is the independence of Kosova and Ohrid Agreement in FYROM that have made possible the departure of Serbian administration and repressive machinery from Kosova and preserves (fragile and often the subject of manipulation) the peace between Albanians and Slavo-Macedonians.

On 28th November 2012, Albania celebrated its centennial independence anniversary. The number of the Albanians raising the national flag freely in Tirana, Prishtina or Shkup (Skopje) was surprising. On the occasion the Albanian political leaders met together and in unison expressed their concern about the ANQ, yet to be resolved, which led to the resurfacing of (un) founded fears from regional and neighboring countries.

Naturally, one could ask, is there still an "Albanian question"? If so, what is it? Does it aim at uniting all Albanians in one state by redrawing existing borders in the Balkans? Neighboring countries as well as certain circles outside the region see it that way and boast the frightening consequences.[11] They say that Albanian aspirations for greater political status, human and property rights is the pretext toward the creation of Greater Albania which will set off a "domino effect" in the region and in the wider world.

It is therefore clear that the ANQ is yet far from resolution. As such, this paper describes the causes of nationalism in the Western Balkans and argues that 19th Century nationalist platforms of Albania's neighbors, which are still at work today, are the main causes of instability in the area. Then analyzes the origins of Albanian nationalism as well as argue that there is no central force or national platform by the Albanians, which aims at establishing a Greater Albania. Finally it assesses the role that Albania plays in solving its national question.

Nationalism in Western Balkans

In his book *Nationalism*, Peter Alter argues that "nationalism is one of the most ambiguous concepts in the present day vocabulary of political and analytical thought."[12] "It is something very new and yet frequently a reformulation of many older ideas with altered meanings and understandings."[13] According to the philosopher and social anthropologist Ernest Gellner, "It is primarily an ideology, whose proponents advocate the indispensable congruence of the political and the national unit, e.g., the state and the nation."[14]

However, the majority of definitions in use have four common features of nationalism: the uniqueness of the people based on language, ethnicity and religion, common socio-cultural values and common history, and contempt amounted to pure hatred toward other people.

In his book *Ethnic Politics in Eastern Europe*, Janusz Bugajski describes three principal forms of nationalism in Western Balkans: *Territorial Self Determination, Separatism,* and *Irredentism.*[15] According to Bugajski the first form that of *Territorial Self*

4

Determination, is visible among reasonably large, well organized, and territorially compact ethnic group or subgroups in a state where they form a relative or absolute majority of the population [e.g., Rep. Srpska, Bosnia]. *Separatism* is characteristic among ethnically and territorially compact populations who openly oppose continuing inclusion in the existing federal or unitary state or are fearful of increasing centralization and campaign to create their own independent state structures [e.g., Kosova]. Finally, *Irredentism* describes a separatist movement in one state seeking to join their territories and populations with nearby state structure, either as an autonomous region or as an integral administrative unit. In some instances the movement gains tacit or direct support by a neighboring state seeking to expand its own borders (e.g., Greek Minority in South Albania).

There is an erroneous belief that nationalism is a product of the Balkans xenophobia or ancient hatred.[16] However, if one is to analyze the roots of this culture, one is to discover that nationalism naturally stems from Western Europe. When it spread in Southeastern Europe the mass civic democratic political type of nationalism mutated into an ethno-linguistic type model where the only criteria of potential nationhood centered on ethnicity and language.[17]

Ideological factors and academic/religious interpretations of history have an enormous influence in Balkans.[18] Serbian and Greek nationalists worked feverishly to implant false national histories in the minds of the individuals targeted by the territories in which they lived. By pointing to places of historical events and erecting monuments upon them, nationalists, in both countries, re-invented the past to fit conveniently with perceptions of historical injustice[19] as well as to convince members of the nation, and

5

indeed themselves that such historical events were, in fact, the history of the nation. The places existed in reality, therefore, the events and all their fabricated nuances were true too.[20] Thus, "the significance of national narratives for Serbia and Greece explains the outcome of conflicting claims that are generated by more or less selective references to, and interpretations of, written and oral historical narratives, a process that establishes collective beliefs in the legitimacy of claims to a territorial motherland."[21] Through romantic revisionism of history the Serbian and Greek nationalists described minorities as outsiders who migrated into national territories. Therefore, the ruling nation had the right to expel or assimilate minorities as it saw fit.[22]

In fact, irredentism after the end of the Ottoman Empire, which continues even nowadays in the Balkans, was probably the most important determinant of how Serbian and Greek states behaved and developed in the Balkans. The demarcation of the Balkan frontiers was instrumental in the rise of ethnic conflicts and exemplified irredentism.[23] Serbia and Greece have seized opportunities repeatedly.[24] In this case Albanians suffered the most.

The Serbian claims over Albania were the most important for the ANQ because they claimed more than half of the Albanian space. The Program (*Načertanije*), a geo-political plan drawn up in 1844 by Ilija Garašanin, the leader of the Serbian Constitutionalist Party, saw the newly autonomous Serbia as nothing but the nucleus of the future revived medieval empire of the Tsar Dušan.[25] Garašanin glorified Serbia's medieval past and speculated on a revival of Serbia's fortune. He recognized that Serbian expansion meant annexation of other people's territories in the Balkans, including Kosova[26] and northern Albania. The latter was of particular interest because it

6

would give Serbia an outlet to the Adriatic Sea that was a necessity to prevent an Austrian monopoly over Serbian foreign trade.

In pursuit of the Garašanin plan Serbia exercised total control over schools, including textbooks and curriculum to convey better Serbian nationalist message. Serbian texts were full with myths[27] and tales of heroic martyrs who killed or died for Serbia and Kosova. Through these patriotic books and teachers, such accounts influenced and continue to influence Serbian elite and population.[28]

The most comprehensive platform against Albanians came from Vaso Čubrilovič, who was a historian at Belgrade University and a member of the Serbian Cultural Club. In his long policy paper, entitled *"The expulsion of the Arnauts"* he argued that "At a time when Germany can expel tens of thousands of Jews, and Russia transplants millions of people from one part of the continent to another, the shifting of a few hundred thousand Albanians will not lead to the outbreak of a world war.*"[29]*

In 1986 the Serbian Academy of Sciences and Arts compiled another platform to deal with Albanians. The platform entitled *"On the political, economic and constitutional position of Serbia in the Yugoslav Federation"* gave fuel to Serbian nationalism by artificially distorting the facts and altering the number of population in Kosova in which according to them "Kosova will not have any Serb in 10 years time."[30] By this time, the extreme Serbian nationalists in Belgrade recommended not merely the absorption of Kosova into a Greater Serbia, but the physical expulsion of Albanians from the province.[31] In 1998-1999 the International Community witnessed with horror of the expulsion in biblical proportion of a million Albanians from Kosova by the Serbian repressive machinery and thousands of civilians killed on behalf of the "sacred" right over the 'cradle of Serbia'.

After the liberation of Greece, Ioannis Koletis the first Prime Minister of Greece at that time, though not an ethnic Greek but a Vlach,[32] made a call for the uniting of all Greek-speaking lands, and the so-called Great Idea (Megali Idea), had been born. [33] The Megali Idea envisioned not only the acquisition of territories, in which Greeks were dominant nationality but also of ethnically mixed lands for which they could put forward historic, geographic, cultural, and strategic claims. The Greek's Megali Idea virtually envisaged the resurrection of the ancient Byzantium. The peculiar aspects of the Megali Idea and the goals of Greek nationalism has been uncertainty what is considered Greek, and why. Greek nationalist deliberately confused religious affiliation with the Greek Orthodox Church with ethnicity. [34] According to Eleftherios Venizelos, the former prime minister of Greece, "neither race, nor language, nor skull could be used as the basis for determining the nationality and that national conscience must be the overriding factor."[35] The result has been conflict with Albania over South Epirus (Çamëria, Northern Greece) and Northern Epirus (Southern Albania).[36]

Greece refused to recognize Albanian independence until 1923, more than 10 years after most states. In the aftermath of World War I, Greece considered all Albanian Muslims in Çamëria as Turks, and therefore transferred them to Turkey with other Turkish nationals, following the international treaty signed between the two states in 1923 at Lausanne. World War II saw many of these issues resurface. Consistent with the model, the conflicts arose from the competing ethno-territorial claims to areas where overlapping population pockets, extensive external Greek support, and Albanian state weakness were all salient.[37]

The Megali Idea continues to play a significant role in Greece's politics, even today. "Just as the nationalism constructs history on its own terms, it also constructs enslaved fellow ethnics in enemy territory."[38] Greece and their leaders consistently want to liberate the "unredeemed" Greeks abroad [e.g., Northern Epirus]. For internal political considerations it is difficult for any political leader in Athens to either appear to abandon unredeemed Greeks or not lend at least verbal support to the cause. Under these circumstances, the Greek Orthodox Church and political positions become impossible to separate.[39]

In a visit to Albania's capital in January 1991, Constantine Mitsotakis, the Greek Prime Minister, urged Albanian citizens of Greek origin not to abandon their homes in Albania to seek a better life abroad for Greece thereupon will be their protector.[40] In May 1994, Bishop Sevastianos of Konitsa, in Northern Greece, asked that tanks be sent in South Albania (northern Epirus).[41]

The Greek efforts to 'Hellenize' Southern Albania have continued, relentlessly.[42] The most conspicuous action was by one of Archbishop Anastasios's aides who disseminated maps and other information in Southern Albania; as well as the 1995 arrest of five Albanians, of Greek origin, on the suspicion of activities against the Albanian state. A powerful reaction outside the Greek State came from the Greek Lobby in the United States, headed by Nicholas Gage, who is the president of the Greek Community in America.[43]

9

Under the influence of the Greek Lobby and uninformed about the real situation in Albania, powerful men in the U.S. National Security Council and the Senate bought into the Greek lobby propaganda. Former United States ambassador in Albania, Joseph E. Lake would characterize the actions taken by these men as an "equivalent of guerrilla warfare" toward Albania.[44] The net result, for a while was that Albania was qualified as an anti-American country that supports terrorism and a "no-go" country for the American citizens. It is by this time that the respected *CIA World Fact-Book* artificially raised the number of Greeks in Albania to 400,000 thousand, a number of in accordance with Greek claims.

Greece and Serbia often have joined their efforts against Albanians. During the conflict in Kosova in 1998-1999 the massive expulsion of Kosovar Albanians was under-estimated by the Greek media industry, which emphasized instead the future danger posed by Greater Albania.[45] According to opinion polls published during that period, 96-98 percent of the Greek public opposed the NATO air campaign against Serbia.[46] The Greeks are obsessed with everything American and Muslim to the extent of paranoia. According to a poll with secondary school students, conducted by the Greek National Centre of Social Research, who were asked to rank nations according to their preferences showed that Albanians and Turks together with Americans ranked at the bottom of the list—even lower than the Roma. The Serbs were in first place as most admired.[47]

The anti-Albanian sentiment also runs deep in the Greek Armed Forces. Disregarding that Albania is an ally in NATO, Greek military personnel chanted anti-Albanian calls during a military parade in March 2011.[48] A year earlier, in March 2010, the Greek newspaper "Ta Nea" published news reporting that YouTube broadcast a video cast featuring hate songs against Albanians. The video presented a platoon of Greek soldiers chanting: "We will make shoelaces with the intestines of the Albanians" or "We will slaughter them until they worship the cross."[49]

Greece, although falsely maintaining it support for Albanian integration into the EU, makes maximum efforts to achieve its policy objectives found in the infamous Megali Idea, by pressuring [50] Albanian politicians into accepting things that they otherwise would not do. By camouflaging their irredentist calls with EU flavor, Greece openly interferes with Albanian internal affairs. The latest example of proof that Megali Idea is alive is the Greek consul action in the city of Korça (South Albania) during the preparation of the census in Albania. In a meeting with Omonia, the organization that represents the Greek minority in Albania, he openly said "Korça has Greeks that should not fear declaring themselves, your grandparents were Greeks. Our struggle starts with the registration of the Greek people that are present here." [51]

The Myth of Greater Albania

On the occasion of the Centennial Anniversary of Independence the Albanian Prime Minister Sali Berisha stated that "Ismail Qemal Vlora in 1912 declared the independence of Albania from Preveza to Presheva and from Skopje to Podgorica." The statement immediately drew the ire of Greece and Macedonia. Macedonian president Ivanov refused the invitation from Albanian president Nishani to participate in the celebration, without explicit reasons.[52] The Greek Foreign minister, at the last minute, canceled the visit he had planned on the occasion.[53] In addition, Greek members of the European Parliament went on to declare that "It is clear that such statements undermine the progress of Albania in Europe and damage good neighborly relations in the

11

region,"[54] signaling the often repeated 'threat' that Albania's path into the EU is through Greece. Various op-eds from the region's media, and beyond, commented on the declaration. What all had in common was the prospect and the danger of Greater Albania.

The threat emanating from Greater Albania is often mentioned in academic, political, and diplomatic circles . This has been particularly the case from the early 1990s and on when the ANQ in the Balkans came to the fore. Serbia, in particular, has been very active in spreading propaganda about the danger posed by the prospect of Greater Albania. The term, alien to the Albanians, was first coined when Serbia and Greece and other Balkan states declared war on the Ottoman Empire in 1912 when it was on the brink of collapse and just had accepted the Albanian demand to merge four Albanian villayets into one. Fearing a rise in Albanian nationalism they joined efforts to 'put a halt to Greater Albania claims'.[55]

What is interesting though is that the term, since its invention has been used whenever Serbs perceived that their colonizing status over the Albanians in former Yugoslavia was threatened.[56] Plot theories involving Russia,[57] in the 1980s, a production of the irredentist materials by the former communist regime in Albania,[58] to the alleged training camps of the Kosova Liberation Army run by Iranians,[59] all centered on degrading and discrediting, in the eyes of the West, the Albanian national cause. Greece often for its own interest and in concert with Serbia has followed suit.[60]

Western media, in general, often bases its views on the Albanians in rush and on stereotypes that lack details and are laden with euphemisms.[61] "The problem of a greater Albania is not in the fact of whether it is real or not. The problem is that the myth exists, the perception exists. As soon as the Albanians mention the issue of the borders or the flag, it is perceived as a part of a greater Albania plot."[62]

However, for Albanians, despite of their living place, the term "Greater Albania" is alien.[63] Instead, they use the term "Ethnic Albania" or "Albanian Space" that implies a region in which the Albanian language and culture are dominant within the political parameters of a unified Europe.[64] This definition appeals to moderate Albanians as it avoids the issue of border changes and difficulties with the Helsinki Final Act and its provisions. As the former Albanian President Rexhep Meidani said on one occasion "the task of Albanians in the Balkans is not to change borders, but to open them."[65] Despite that, the myth about "Ethnic Albania" is not that powerful[66] (as is The Battle of Kosova myth for the Serbs), there are many in political and academic circles in the West who often express their fear[67] of such nationalist ideal as well as push the neighboring countries into a kind of an ad hoc coalition against Albanians.[68]

Several factors play down this fear. Primarily, the Albanians' lack of a nationalist consciousness compares with that of its neighbors. Albanian nationalism came very late into being. Albanian nationalism traces its roots initially to 1878 when the Albanian League of Prizëren (Lidhja Shqiptare e Prizërenit) came into being. Albanian nationalists were quite moderate in their request toward the "Ottoman Porte". They requested autonomy under the suzerainty of Sultan. In addition, Ottoman administration hampered Albanian nationalism by refusing to recognize that Albanians had a distinct identity of their own different from that of the Turks.[69] The massive proselytizing of Albanians from Christianity to Islam during 17 and 18 Century as well as the role held by prominent Albanians in political and military circles in the Ottoman administration led

13

to a general identification of the Albanians with the Turks[70], which ensured that Albanians became the last nation in the region to gain independence from the Ottomans in 1912.

In addition, Albanians remained fragmented and unable to establish a unifying or central authority that would have commanded their collective allegiance. Except from the Albanians, other nations in the region enjoyed a distinct religious homogeneity. The foreign propagandists exploited the difference in religion among the Albanians through their churches to spread suspicion and distrust to further their anti – Albanian designs.[71] This is why the Albanians lack the identity comparable to that which produced the notions of Greater Serbia and Greater Greece.[72]

Moreover, Albanians have never lived in one state except for a short period during the Fifteenth Century, under Gjergj Kastrioti, Skënderbeu (George Castrioti, or Scanderbeg in English). Today, Albanians "have got used to the idea of separate Albanian entities in the Balkans and are therefore, content to preserve their separate political identities as long as business, cultural and travel restrictions are removed."[73]

Finally, the national question has created a paradoxical situation in Albanian visualization of nationhood because almost all accept that "we are one nation," but concerning the unification majority of them excludes this possibility. The national question seems to be something very distant that does not affect their daily lives; perhaps it was a good idea in the past, or in the future, but it has nothing to do with them in the present.[74]

It can be argued, therefore that the threat of Greater Albania is more a myth than reality as Albanians themselves have no political agendas and do not want to live in one state. According to the International Crises Group (ICG), the "Greater Albania issue is inexistent in the political agendas of Albania, Kosova and elsewhere."[75] The specter of Greater Albania is more of chimera than a challenge to regional stability [76] because Albania lacks the power or outside support to put a credible irredentist claim on its neighbors.

The Albanian nation position has changed over the past decade. Kosova declared its independence from Serbia in 2008. In Macedonia the Albanian political parties participate in the government. Albania is a member of NATO and its relative position in the region is growing. In general, time is working for the Albanians in the Balkans, contrary to Serbia's and Greece's predictions and efforts to halt it. However, there are voices that make dark predictions for the Albanians future who wish the decline of the American power and its influence in the region, to settle, once and for all, problems with the Albanians in "a messy and unpleasant, in the distinctly Balkan way."[77]

Despite what goes on officially, there are Albanian politicians and scholars that stress that the national unification should happen. The Albanian Academy of Sciences, published in 1998, a controversial paper in which it interpreted the ANQ as"*the movement for the liberation of Albanian lands from foreign occupation and their unification into one national state.*"[78] After its publication, it drew appraisals and criticisms alike. Many analysts in Albania voiced their concern on the impracticality of that platform.[79]

In addition, new parties with espoused nationalist profiles have come into the political scene. The "Vetëvendosje" (self-determination) political party in Kosova and "Aleanca Kuq e Zi" (Red and Black Alliance) in Albania advocate the unification of

Albanian lands into one state. Furthermore, another party that promotes the Albanian Çams rights in Greece currently participates in the Albanian Parliament. What is interesting though is that none of them foresees the redrawing of the Balkan borders. The statement of the Macedonian academic, Ljobomir Frckoski, fits well with political behavior of certain Albanian parties and politicians "When you deal with politicians in the Balkans, you need at least two guide books. One is to explain what they really mean when they say something; and another, which is heavier, to explain what they really intend to do after all."[80] Their discourse is focused to Albanian audiences to raise the number of votes for the political election. Upon satisfaction of partial requests, very soon they have abandoned their national unification discourse to replace it with the stabilization of the state in which they are residing. [81]

The advocates of national unification limit themselves to the point of the debate whether the unification and the creation of one state is needed or not. The question of how the unification will become reality and its ramification has never come to the fore. [82] Simple factors such as the form of government (unitary, federal or other), economy, monetary policy, legal system, and the list may go are never discussed and often overlooked. Reaction of neighbor countries (Montenegro, Macedonia, Greece, Serbia, Serbs in Kosova) is not factored into the calculus despite the fact the unification moves will lead certainly to bloodshed.

It is true that the massive exodus of almost half a million Albanian Kosovar refugees in 1999 played a significant role in strengthening community ties among people. Albanians, throughout the Albanian space, became conscious that together they constituted an important factor in the regional power balance that could not be ignored.

[83] In addition, the construction of highways, free movement of people and goods, telecommunication expansion, and cultural interaction have all contributed to fostering close ties within Albanian communities in the region.

All these developments unsettle neighboring countries that interpret everything that happens with plans to create Greater Albania. Infrastructure projects[84] or proposals to create a Balkan Benelux or ALMAKOSMO (Albania, Macedonia, Kosova, and Montenegro) were vehemently put down as an expression toward creating Greater Albania.[85] Serbs rushed to play it down because "this would be an Albanian, rather than a Balkan Benelux, because of the exclusion of Serbia."[86]

Only by taking in account several of these elements as well as practical difficulties, the national unification remains a distant dream destined to remain as such even if 100 % of the Albanian people support it enthusiastically. When asked about the Greater Albania issue, the Albanian ambassador at the United Nations declared that "In no occasion Albania has had, has or will have any plan, platform, open or secret, in which it discusses the changes of borders in the Balkans. In contrary, this would be detrimental to Albania's interest because in this way it will lose its biggest ally, the USA."[87]

Moreover, the International Community, despite its divisions, is in unison, and pressure Albanians to consider their national question as a closed matter. In this framework the regions' integration into the European Union is a substitute formula, where the borders will lose relevance and where the language of nationalism and self determination is practically a thing of the past.

In sum, there is no agenda or a platform, steered by a central authority, pushing toward creation of a Greater Albania because of the many factors mentioned above. One should agree with Kola's conclusion that *"...I looked to find the "Greater Albania" in history and nowadays but could not find it."*[88]

The Role of the Republic of Albania

Albania has never been in a position which would decisively promote the ANQ despite being seen as the mother country from Albanians living outside its political borders.[89] First, lacking the support from powerful allies similarly with its neighbors, Albania's major concern has been to safeguard its independence in the face of constant threats from its hostile Balkan neighbors.[90] The safest way to achieve the goal was not to get involved in the ANQ. Second, the Albanian political class, since the foundation of the state in 1913, has often lacked the ability to put forward a united vision of national interest.[91] Internal political power struggles often contributed to damaging the national question; thus, giving its neighbors, whose interest were aligned with Great Powers, another reason to claim what was not theirs and Great Powers to ignore and not take seriously, any Albanian demand. This confusion has led to the creation by Serbia and Greece, fearful of the change of Albanian political status, and a relative shift of power in South-eastern Europe, of the evil Greater Albania image, aimed at outlawing, morally and legally, solving of the ANQ.[92]

The Albanian state, recognized by the Great Powers in the London Conference of 1913, came out with a shattered national, political, and economic cohesion. The period of 1913-1919 was characterized by widespread instability because of the Great War; the country became a battleground of foreign armies. There was no viable central government when the country was struggling to survive. King Zogu I (1928-1939),

18

adopted an 'Albania only' [emphasis added] policy in the face a military threat posed by its neighbors. He consistently suppressed the Albanian patriots who advocated the armed struggle[93] for Kosova and was forced to dilute his nationalistic stance toward Greece, regarding Çamëria, when faced with the harsh realities of Albania's economic and political situation.[94]

The communist, except for a short time during the wartime period, 1939-1944, in which advocated the solving of national question, betrayed the ANQ in the interests of the stability of the regime in Tirana. The Communist elite, realizing their regime weakness, proceeded to forge a close alliance with Tito's Yugoslavia, agreeing to shelve the Kosova question.[95] Albanian foreign policy was generally narrow, hesitant, and conservative in its attitude toward the ANQ, in general.[96] For the next 40 — plus years, Albania sought alliances designed to ensure the territorial integrity of the Albanian state[97].

In 1991, the collapse of Communism in Albania and the disintegration of Yugoslavia contributed to Albanian Foreign Policy becoming more assertive toward solving the ANQ.[98] The Kosova problem was by far the most important element in Albanian Foreign Policy, from 1991-1997 with its capacity to draw Albania into war with Serbia and into the heart of the Balkan crisis. Nevertheless, prevention of the conflict remained the dominant concern. A possible conflict with Serbia over Kosova would have proved catastrophic for Albania that could have not successfully defended itself."[99] In addition, the country was experiencing a difficult economic transition toward capitalism and free market and was aware that efforts to change borders by military

19

force would cause a bloodbath and lose its essential and desperately needed foreign assistance.[100]

Concerning Macedonia, Tirana welcomed the formation of the new state, primarily because it considered it as a counterweight to Serbia and Greece and urged the Albanians of Macedonia to remain calm.[101] Although the Macedonian authorities failed to address any of the Albanian grievances—e.g., human rights— Albania was among the first states to recognize Macedonia. It did not pursue the issue of human rights energetically because Macedonia was not a central issue in Albanian politics, and it seemed that Albania's position compared favorably with the very bad conditions endured by the Albanians in Serbian-ruled Kosova.

The 1997 instability in Albania, following the collapse of Ponzi Schemes, caused the cessation of Albania's role as a factor in Balkan politics as well as reframed inter-Albanian relations. During the communist era, Albanians, on both sides of the border, had little or no communication because of the poor relationship that existed between Albania and the former Yugoslavia. The lack of communication for this long period led the Albanians outside Albania to have an idealistic view of Albania and its dictator Enver Hoxha. Albania's break with communism and its emergence into international life and the transition to democracy was painful. Thereafter, many Kosovar/Macedonian Albanians realized that Albania could not and would not be their country.[102]

Following the 1997 elections, the Albanian government had no 'specific' policy on how to address the ANQ and the ex-communist ruling elite was often not really fully in touch with events in Albanian space. The only commitment demonstrated by Albania to the national cause was rhetorical.[103] Hostilities in 1998-1999 in Kosova forced Tirana to change its policy. However, it would have been highly controversial for the government to be seen to stop KLA activity anywhere in Albania. In the interests of 'national solidarity', therefore, the Tirana authorities turned a blind eye to the activities of Kosovar insurgents in Albania. The NATO intervention and subsequent expulsion of the Serbian repression machine in May 1999 closed an important chapter of the Albanian national question.

The outbreak of the conflict in Macedonia in 2001 caught Albania completely unprepared and showed the extent to which the political establishment in Tirana was out of tune with the growing Albanian frustration in Macedonia. There was no policy in place to deal with the problem. The Ministry of Foreign Affairs issued several statements where the government pledged its support for Macedonia security and urged Albanian guerrillas to lay down arms and seek a peaceful solution. In sum, during the conflict in Macedonia, Albania did play a minor role in helping to solve the problem. The only role it played was to the detriment of the NLA cause as she deployed troops on the border to disrupt the alleged supply lines from Albania. [104]

The Çam issue[105] has been a taboo subject in Albanian foreign policy. Throughout the cold war period the perpetuation of a climate of hostility in Greek - Albanian relations, particularly through constant rekindling of the minorities' question, served the needs of both sides for regime stabilization in the face of domestic opponents via the projection of enemy images of a hostile and aggressive neighboring state.[106] In the early years, after the collapse of communism, the issue remained silent given the 'preferential' and 'influential' role that Greece played in Albania's domestic and foreign policy making.

However, the issue came up in the political agenda after a publication by the British Defense Academy in 2002[107] and a heated debate followed in Parliament, without any result. The only formal attempt of the Albanian state was a so-called Parliament resolution in 2004, in the form of a formal request to the Greek Parliament to start negotiations over the Çam problem. This resolution was agreed upon the first day to be rejected in the next, by left wing parties to appease the Greeks. To date the Çam issue remains on hold because of Albania's inability to influence Greek Government[108] and the strong pressure exerted by Greece that whenever possible, plays the EU integration card, [109] and the Albanian emigrants in Greece, as a powerful instrument of its foreign policy toward Albania.

In sum Albania's role in solving the ANQ is not similar to that of a mother country that is following an 'agreed upon' platform. The impetus for change did not come because of Tirana's foreign policy but from Albanians in Kosova and Macedonia and Çams yet to come. Because Albania has never shown capacity to accomplish its responsibility as the mother country, the Tirana political elite have not and cannot play a central role in solving the ANQ.[110] Lulzim Basha, former Albanian Foreign Minister has explained that: "Tirana is keeping quiet about the Albanian minority outside its borders because it has been directed to act so by the United States and the European Union Even if we were to disregard this advice, it would hurt more than help. Tirana's too weak to do much...even diplomatically."[111]

Conclusions

In conclusion, nationalism is not a phenomenon inherently linked with the Balkans. One has to find its roots in 19th century Western Europe attempts to create societies of equal citizens based on human values. However, in the Balkans the notion of nationalism was distorted to fulfill the xenophobic agendas of the newly established states, Serbia, and Greece. Since their inception, the Serbian, and Greek governments were irredentist. Nationalist governments of both countries, supported by the religious leaders, developed national narratives based on selected readings, and sometimes wrong interpretations, of history, and lies to help defend their claims and their 'historical rights' of a more 'civilized people'[112] toward Albanian inhabited lands.

To satisfy their demands, Greek, and Serbian elites, created infamous platforms and plans against other peoples' in the region and in particular, against the Albanians who, with the demise of Ottoman Empire, experienced an unrelenting hostility by its aggressive neighbors who often joined their efforts to physically annihilate, expulse or assimilate them.

Until the late 1990s, the Albanian question was largely unknown to Western Europe but a few academic circles. In most of the cases, Albanians are portrayed in the West through Serbian and Greek lenses that have given, to a large extent, the wrong perception of what the Albanians want. The danger posed by the alleged Greater Albania scheme, skillfully propagated by the Slav and Greek propaganda machinery, to a certain extent exacerbated and helped to demonize and morally downgrade the Albanian question. In a concerted disinformation campaign, Albania's neighbors, and unfortunately some academic and government circles in the West, with strong ties with Slav and Greek agendas deliberately have exaggerated the risk emanating from the alleged Greater Albania.

However, one can easily conclude that this is far from the truth. Today, political pragmatism exists among the majority of Albanian elites. Moreover, Albanians

23

themselves are more concerned with their economic development and the right to move without restrictions and preserve cultural and family ties while respecting political borders. There is little enthusiasm from Albanians to pursue the project of Greater Albania in an unstable region with a blood stained past. Albania's president has declared that "Albania does not have any open problem with any of the regional states. Particurlary Albania and the Albanians have never had interests which threatens the integrity of negboring countries." [113]

Albania's influence over events in Albanian space (Kosova, Macedonia, Montenegro, Serbia, Greece, and elsewhere) is much more symbolic than real. The Albanian role in solving the ANQ is not similar with that of Serbia and Greece where from the position of the mother country it pursues an agreed agenda. "All [ethnic] Albanian [political] centers make decisions autonomously: Tirana, Prishtina, Tetova, etc. None of the ethnic Albanian members of the Macedonian parliament are directed from Tirana or Prishtina; the same is true for the members of the Kosova Assembly." [114]

To the other states in the Balkans, Albanian nationalism may pose a threat. The large numbers of Albanians outside Albania represent a possible and even a real irredentism threat for years to come. For Albania, their anxiety over becoming engulfed in conflict has preoccupied their time with 'a consolidation and purification of national identity', in other words, with maintenance of their present boundaries. [115]

In addition, the existing geo-political conditions in the region, and associated relative Albanian state weakness, diminish the role and the influence that Albania could exert amongst Albanians in the region. Although Albanians would like to see what they consider as a great historical injustice redressed, political elites in Tirana similar to

24

International Community accept and proclaim the sanctity of existing borders in the region. The hope is that rather than aiming to change borders there is no need for barriers between Albanians. In a mongrel world, ethnically pure states are, for the most part, a practical impossibility without endless war and unthinkable transfers of population. It is not that people should live together; it is that they have to. There is no other way.[116]

Endnotes

[1] Vansitart minute, 5/12/1913, FO371/1823/54900 quoted in Nicola Guy, *The Birth of Albania: Ethnic Nationalism, the Great Powers of World I and the Emergence of Albanian Independence* (New York: IB Tauris & Co Ltd, 2012), 62.

[2] Michas, Takis, *Unholy Alliance: Greece and Milosevic's Serbia* (Texas: A&M University Press, 2002), XIII.

[3] James Der Derian, "International Theory, Balkanization and New World Order", *Millenium: Journal of International Studies* 20, no.3 (1991):488.

[4] Great Powers before 1st World War included, Great Britain, Germany, France, Austro-Hungary, Russia and Italy.

[5] Miranda Vickers, *The Albanians: A modern History* (London: I.B.Tauris, 1999), 97.

[6] Nicola Guy, *The Birth of Albania: Ethnic Nationalism, the Great Powers of World I and the Emergence of Albanian Independence* (New York: IB Tauris & Co Ltd, 2012), 17.

[7] Lord Grey quoted in Nicola Guy, *The Birth of Albania: Ethnic Nationalism, the Great Powers of World I and the Emergence of Albanian Independence* (New York: IB Tauris & Co Ltd, 2012), 62.

[8] Gazmen Xhudo, *Diplomacy and Crisis Management in the Balkans: A US foreign Policy Perspective* (NY: ST. Martin's Press, Inc. 1996), 109.

[9] Dana H. Allin, "The Western Alliance and its Balkan Protectorates", *Adelphi Papers* 42, no. 347 (2002): 75.

[10] James Pettifer and Miranda Vickers, *The Albanian Question* (London: I.B Taurus, 2007), 166.

[11] Bat Juddy ed., "Is there any Albanian Question", *Chaillot Paper*, no.107 (Jan 2008): 5.

[12] Quoted in Boriana Marinova – Zuber, "The Rebirth of Nationalism in the Balkans in the 1990s: Causes, Consequences and Possible Solutions", *ISR Network* (August 2007): 5.

[13] George W. White, *Nationalism and Territory: Constructing Group identity in Southeastern Europe* (USA: Rowaman & Littlefield Publishers, Inc, 2000), 251.

[14] Ernest, Gellner, *Nations and Nationalism* (Oxford: Basil Blackwell, 1983), 1.

[15] Janusz, Bugajski, *Ethnic Politics in Eastern Europe* (USA: M.E.Sharpe, 1995), 20-30.

[16] William W. Hagen, "The Balkans' Lethal Nationalisms", *Foreign Affairs* (July, 1999 / August, 1999):52

[17] D.A. Smith, *Nationalism and Modernism* (London: Routledge, 1998) quoted in Bledar Meti, Greek Nationalism and the Scope of its Interrelationship with Albania (UK: AuthorHousetm UK Ltd, 2010), 20.

[18] Pettifer and Vickers, *The Albanian Question*, 261.

[19] Andre Gerolymatos, *The Balkan Wars* (USA: Basic Books, 2002), 1.

[20] White, *Nationalism and Territory: Constructing Group Identity in Southeastern Europe*, 253.

[21] Victor Roudomentof, Collective Memory, National Identity, and Ethnic Conflict (USA: Praeger Publishers, 2002), 16.

[22] White, *Nationalism and Territory: Constructing Group Identity in Southeastern Europe*, 60.

[23] G. Kritikos, "The Geography of Nationalisms and Human Security in the Pre-Communist Balkan Space", *Southeast European and Black Sea Studies* 11, no. 4 (2011):394

[24] M. Wiener, "Matching Peoples, Territories and States: Post-Ottoman Irredentism in the Balkans and in the Middle East," ed., D. Elazar, *Governing peoples and Territories* (Tel Aviv: Jerusalem Institute for Federal Studies, 1982), quoted in David S. Siroky, *Secession and Survival: Nations, States and Violent Conflict* (USA: ProQuest LLC, 2009), 143.

[25] Thanasis Sfikas and Christopher Williams, *Ethnicity and Nationalism in East Central Europe and the Balkans* (UK: Antony Rowe Ltd, 1999), 30.

[26] In the paper Albanian language place names will be used, e.g. Kosova not Kosovo, although the   latter form is more common in some sections of international community. However, whenever deemed necessary the place names will appear in both languages, e.g. Prishtina / Pristina.

[27] On the Serbian manipulation of history read Noel Malcolm, *Kosovo: A Short History* (London: Papermac, 1998), 26, 41, 46, 50, 159 and 256.

[28] Steven Sowards "The Balkans in the Age of Nationalism,*"* http://www.lib.msu.edu/sowards/balkan (accessed 15 Nov 2012).

[29] Philip Cohen, *Serbia's Secret War: Propaganda and the Deceit of History* (USA: A&M University press, 1996), 5-10.

[30] See Serbian Academy of Science and Arts, *On the Political, Economic and Constitutional Position of Serbia in the Yugoslav Federation* (Belgrade: Duga, 1986), 55.

[31] James Pettifer, *Kosova Express* (UK: C.Hurst & Co Publishers, 2005), 34.

[32] The Vlachs known as 'Vllah' in Albanian language are remnants of an assimilated pastoral population that are dispersed in the entire Balkan Peninsula. Their origin is claimed equally by the Greeks, Macedonians and the Romanians based on religious and to a lesser extent language background.

[33] Bledar Meti, *Greek Nationalism and the Scope of its Interrelationship with Albania* (UK: AuthorHouse[tm] UK Ltd, 2010), 25.

[34] Elez Biberaj, *Albania in Transition-The Rocky Road to Democracy* (USA: Westview Press, 1998), quoted in Bledar Meti, *Greek Nationalism and the Scope of its Interrelationship with Albania* (UK: AuthorHouse[tm] UK Ltd, 2010), 33.

[35] Guy, *The Birth of Albania: Ethnic Nationalism, the Great Powers of World I and the Emergence of Albanian Independence*, 167.

[36] Steven Sowards, "The Balkans in the Age of Nationalism," http://www.lib.msu.edu/sowards/balkan (accessed 12 November 2012).

[37] Siroky, *Secession and Survival: Nations, States and Violent Conflict*, 189.

[38] Angelo Ellefantis, " Apo tin Ethnikistiki Exarsi sto Perithorio" quoted in Michas, Takis, *Unholy Alliance: Greece and Milosevic's Serbia* (Texas : A&M University Press, 2002),54.

[39] C.P. Danoppoulos and A. Çopani, "Albanian nationalism and Prospects for Greater Albania" in Constadine P. Danopuolos and Kostas G. Messas, *Crisis in the Balkans: Views from the Participants* (USA: Westview Press 1997), 185.

[40] Gazmen Xhudo, *Diplomacy and Crisis Management in the Balkans: A US foreign Policy Perspective* , 46.

[41] Takis, *Unholy Alliance: Greece and Milosevic's Serbia*, 111.

[42] For background on Greek policy toward Albania see J. Pettifer and M. Vickers, *The Albanian Question: Reshaping the Balkans* (London and New York: I.B. Tauris, 2007); Despite its near collapsed economy the Greek state continues to pay up to 18,000 Albanian citizens, who never worked or were part of Greece's social security system, 330 €uro per month in order to pursue a policy of 'Hellenizing' the population in southern Albania in addition to other incentivization schemes, such as providing EU passports to Albanian citizens who can speak Greek and who profess Orthodox Christianity or funding Greek schools. Greece officials often openly interfere in Albania's internal affairs especially during the election campaigns. They openly urge Albanian citizens of Greek ethnicity to vote for the parties affiliated with Athens

policies toward Albania. The last acts of such interference were the actions of the Greek consul in Korça (South Albania) who openly carried out a campaign to artificially raise the number of Greeks during the Census conducted by Albania last year. A more subtle way that Greece uses in its Hellenizing policy is Greek Orthodox Church. It has usurped the Autocephalous Orthodox Church of Albania by placing in top ranks priests of Greek origin under the pretexts that there is no Albanian clergy ready to take the positions. Moreover, the Albanian state permission to build in its soil several wartime memorials for Greek soldiers killed in Albania during II WW is being used by political parties and Greek Orthodox clergy to make irredentist claims in Southern Albania.

[43] Meti, *Greek Nationalism and the Scope of its Interrelationship with Albania*, 38.

[44] Steven Bucci, *Present at Birth of a Special Relationship: Albania –Dec.1993 through Dec.1995*, Personal Experience Monograph (Carlisle Barracks, PA: U.S, Army War College, 1999), 22.

[45] Takis, *Unholy Alliance: Greece and Milosevic's Serbia*, 13.

[46] Ibid., 79.

[47] Eleftherotypia, December 7, 2000, quoted in Michas, Takis, *Unholy Alliance: Greece and Milosevic's Serbia* (Texas : A&M University Press, 2002),13.

[48] "Këngët antishqiptare në Athinë, nis gjyqi ndaj ushtarëve grekë" [Anti Albanian songs in Athens, starts the trials against Greek soldiers], http://www.zgjohushqiptar.com/2011/09/kenget-antishqiptare-ne-athine-nis.html (accessed 11 Oct 2012).

[49] EU Times, "Greek soldiers chant anti-Turkish-Albanian slogans at military parade", March 29, 2010, http://www.eutimes.net/2010/03/greek-soldiers-chant-anti-turkish-albanian-slogans-at-military-parade/ (accessed 11 Nov 2012).

[50] Gazeta Shekulli, "Panariti's secret report, downed agreement with Greece 'loop in the throat'" 13 Sep 2012, http://www.shekulli.com.al/web/p.php?id=4189&kat=88 (accessed 11 Nov 2012).

[51] Gazeta Bota Sot, "Korçë, Greek Consul: Here is the North Epirus, your grandparents were Greek!" http://www.botasot.info/shqiperia/102552/mfwNyDJ/ (accessed in 11 Nov 2012).

[52] Gazeta Shqip, "Incidentet me Gruevskin, presidenti Ivanov refuzon ftesën e Nishanit për 100 vjetor" [Incidents with Gruevski, president Ivanov refuses Nishani's invitation for 100 anniversary], 27 Nov 2012, http://gazeta-shqip.com/lajme/2012/11/27/incidentet-me-gruevskin-presidenti-ivanov-refuzon-ftesen-e-nishanit-per-100-vjetor/ (accessed 29 Nov 2012).

[53] Balkanweb, "Avramopulos anuloi vizitën, Berisha: Miqtë shkëlqejnë në mungesa", [Avramopulos annuls visits, Berisha: Friends shine during absence], http://www.balkanweb.com/kryesore/1/avramopulos-anuloi-viziten-berisha-miqte-shkelqejne-ne-mungesa-111320.html (accessed 29 Nov 2012).

[54] Balkanweb, "Greek MEP: Berisha statements prevents Albania entrance into EU", http://www.balkanweb.com/rajoni/2687/eurodeputetja-greke-deklarata-e-berishes-pengon-shqiperine-ne-be-111441.html (accessed 30 Nov 2012).

[55] Basilis Kondis, *Greece and Albania in the XX century* (Thessaloniki: n/p, 1997), 44.; Nicola Guy, *The Birth of Albania: Ethnic Nationalism, the Great Powers of World I and the Emergence of Albanian Independence* (New York: IB Tauris & Co Ltd, 2012), 26.

[56] A simple search in Lexis Nexis database with the term "Greater Albania" brings about thousands documents originating from Serbian news agencies dating as back as early 1980s.

[57] Marvine Howe, "Yugoslavs, Shaken By Riots, Fear Plot", *The New York Times*, 27April 1981, Page 3, http://www.lexisnexis.com.ezproxy.usawcpubs.org/hottopics/lnacademic/ (accessed 13 Oct 2012)

[58] Milo Djukic, "Escalation of Albanian Territorial Claims against Yugoslavia", *Yugoslav News Agency*, 10 Jul 86, http://www.lexisnexis.com.ezproxy.usawcpubs.org/hottopics/lnacademic/ (accessed 13 Oct 2012).

[59] TNA, "Serbia: Kosovo's Albanians said to have received guerrilla training in Albania", *Tanjug News Agency*, 7 Mar 1998, http://www.lexisnexis.com.ezproxy.usawcpubs.org/hottopics/lnacademic/, (accessed 13 Oct 2012).

[60] Asteris Huliaras, and Charalambos Tsardanidis, "(Mis) understanding the Balkans: Greek Geopolitical Codes of the Post-communist Era", *Geopolitics* 1, no.3 (2006): 469

[61] Isa Blumi, "The commodification of Otherness and the Ethnic Unit in the Balkans: How to think about Albanians", *East European Politics and Societies* 12, no.3 (1998): 530-531.

[62] Project on Ethnic Relations, *Albanians and their Neighbors: Is the Status Quo Acceptable?* (*Lucerne*: PER, 2002), 35-37.

[63] Miranda Vickers, *The Albanians: A Modern History* (London: I.B.Tauris, 1999), 66.

[64] Pettifer and Vickers, *The Albanian Question*, 238.

[65] Mentor Nazarko ed., *President Rexhep Meidani dhe Kosova* (Tirana: Toena, 2000), 48.

[66] Paskal Milo, *'Greater Albania' - Between Fiction and Reality* (Tirana: n/p, 2001), 20-40.

[67] Project on Ethnic Relations, *Albanians and Their Neighbors: Unfinished Business* (Budapest: PER, 2000), 25.

[68] Ljobomir Frckoski, " Regional Perspectives", in Thanos M. Veremis and Dimitrios Triantaphyllou ed., *Kosovo and The Albanian Dimension in The Southeastern Europe: The Need For Regional Security And Conflict Prevention* (Athens: Hellenic Foundation for European and Foreign Policy, 1999), 159-160.

[69] Guy, *The Birth of Albania: Ethnic Nationalism, the Great Powers of World I and the Emergence of Albanian Independence*, 22.

[70] Vickers, *The Albanians: A Modern History*, 34.

[71] Edwin E. Jacques, *The Albanians: An Ethnic History from Prehistoric Times to the Present (*North Carolina, 1995), 231.

[72] Paulin Kola, *The Myth of Greater Albania* (NY: NY University Press, 2003), 383.

[73] International Crisis Group, "Pan-Albanianism: How Big a Threat to Balkan Stability?", *ICG Report*, 25 Feb 2004, http://www.intl-crisis-group.org (accessed 20 Feb 2013)

[74] Enis Sulstarova, "Hegemony and the Reopening of National Question" in Saras Botime, *Publikja Shqiptare: Ese Kritike, [Albanian Public: Critical Essays]* (Tirana: Saras Botime, 2012) , 55.

[75] Ibid.

[76] R. L. Wolff, *The Balkans in Our Time,* (Massachusetts: Harvard University Press, 1956), quoted in David S. Siroky, *Secession and Survival: Nations, States and Violent Conflict (*USA: ProQuest LLC, 2009), 190.

[77] Srdja Trifkovic, "Macedonia - the new Kosovo", *Jerusalem Post*, 29 Feb 2012, 15.

[78] Akademia e Shkencave të Shqipërisë, *Platformë për Zgjidhjen e Çështjes Kombëtare Shqiptare, [*Albanian Academy of Science, *Platform for the Solution of the ANQ],* (Tirana: Akademia e Shkencave, 1998), 5.

[79] Milo, *'Greater Albania' - Between Fiction and Reality*, 50.

[80] Frckoski, *Kosovo and the Albanian Dimension in the Southeastern Europe: the Need for Regional Security and Conflict Prevention*, 159-160.

[81] Sulstarova, Publikja *Shqiptare: Ese Kritike*, 50.

[82] Gjergj Erebara, "Bashkimi Kombëtar kërkon shumë punë përveç vullnetit", [National Unification requires many work a part of will], Gazeta Shqip, 30 July 2012, http://gazeta-shqip.com/lajme/2012/07/30/bashkimi-kombetar-kerkon-shume-pune-pervec-vullnetit/ (accessed October 30 2012).

[83] Kofos, "The Albanian Question in the Aftermath of the War: A Proposal to Break the Status Deadlock", 156.

[84] "BGj" and "MT", "Does Major Interconnection Come as a Replacement for Greater Albania?", *Dnevnik* , 12 June 2012, 5.

[85] Zoran Dimitrovski, "Benelux in Washington's Agenda", *Nova Makedonija*, Skopje, 7 Jul 1212.

[86] Hristo Ivanovski, "Balkan Benelux Dangerously Smells of Greater Albania", *Dnevnik*, Skopje, 27 Jun 12, 1- 2.

[87] Mr. Ferit Hoxha, Albanian ambassador in UN during Army War College students visit in Albanian Mission in UN, 16 Nov 2012.

[88] Kola, *The Myth of Greater Albania*, 450.

[89] Blendi Kajsiu, Aldo Bumçi, Albert, Rakipi, "Albania - A Weak Democracy A Weak State," *Albanian Institute for International Studies*, www.AIIS.com, (accessed 15 Nov 2012).

[90] Vickers, *The Albanians: A Modern History* 180.

[91] Pettifer and Vickers, *The Albanian Question,* 180.

[92] Rozeta Shembilku, "The 'National Interest' Tradition and the Foreign Policy of Albania", *Fletcher School of Law and Diplomacy*, 2004, http://fletcher.tufts.edu (accessed 10 Sep 2012).

[93] Bernd Fischer, *King Zog and the Struggle for Stability in Albania* (NY: Columbia University Press, 1984), 25.

[94] D. Michalopulos, "The Moslems of Chamouria and the Exchange of Populations between Greece and Turkey", *Balkan Studies* 27, no.2 (1986): 305-6.

[95] Danoppoulos and Çopani, *Crisis in the Balkans: Views from the Participants*, 171.

[96] International Crisis Group, "The View from Tirana: The Albanian Dimension of the Kosovo Crisis", *ICG Report*, 10 July 1998, http://www.intl-crisis-group.org (accessed 20 Feb 2013).

[97] Xhudo, *Diplomacy and Crisis Management in the Balkans: A US foreign Policy Perspective*, 35.

[98] Ibid., *59*

[99] Elez Biberaj, *Albania in Transition* (USA: Westview Press, 1998), 251.

[100] Louis Zanga, "Albania Reduced Total Dependence on Foreign Food", *RFE/RL Reports* 1, no. 8, 21 February 1992.

[101] James Pettifer, *The New Macedonian Question* ed., (GB: Macmillan Press LTD, 1999), 159.

[102] Kola, *The Myth of Greater Albania*, 206.

[103] Maqo Lakrori, " Regional Spillover", in Thanos M. Veremis and Dimitrios Triantaphyllou ed., *Kosovo and the Albanian Dimension in the Southeastern Europe: The Need For Regional*

Security And Conflict Prevention (Athens: Hellenic Foundation for European and Foreign Policy, 1999), 56-58.

[104] John Philips, *Macedonia: Warlords and Rebels in the Balkans* (UK: I.B.Tauris, 2004).181.

[105] The Çams (Chams) were stripped of their property, killed summarily and were expelled from Greece following the Greek Civil War (1946-1949). Earlier, in 1923, under the pretext of population exchange with Turkey the Greek state expelled several thousands of Muslim Albanians towards Turkey. In 1994 Greek government refused to recognize the Çam issue, but latter agreed to provide compensation if the Albanian government would do the same with the property of ethnic Greeks confiscated by the Hoxha regime. Later Greece changed its position and continues to deny that there is any Çam issue. In early 2000 the Çams formed a political Party (PDIU) demanding that they be allowed to return to their properties, or be compensated for their losses by the Greek state.

[106] Thanasis Sfikas and Christopher Williams, *Ethnicity and Nationalism in East Central Europe and the Balkans* (UK: Antony Rowe Ltd, 1999), 178.

[107] On the background of Çam issue read Miranda Vickers, *The Cham Issue - Albanian National & Property Claims in Greece*, CSRC, 2002.

[108] Meti, *Greek Nationalism and the Scope of its Interrelationship with Albania,* 36.

[109] Gazeta Shqip, "Ministria e Jashtme Greke: Nuk ekziston çështja çame, nëse ka pakënaqësi drejtohuni gjykatave greke," [Greek Foreign Affairs Ministry: There is no Cham issue, if there are grievances address the Greek courts], 8 Dec 2012, http://gazeta-shqip.com/lajme/2012/12/08/ministria-e-jashtme-greke-nuk-ekziston-ceshtja-came-nese-ka-pakenaqesi-drejtohuni-gjykatave-greke/ (accessed 8 Dec 2012)

[110] Danoppoulos and Çopani, *Crisis in the Balkans: Views from the Participants*, 186.

[111] Siroky, Secession *and Survival: Nations, States and Violent Conflict*, 165.

[112] Noel Malcolm, *Kosovo: A Short History (*London: Papermac, 1998), XIVIII.

[113] Gazeta Panorama, "Nishani: Nuk kemi probleme në rajon, " [Nishani: We don't have problems in the region], 8 Dec 2012, http://www.panorama.com.al/2012/12/06/nishani-nuk-kemi-probleme-ne-rajon/ (accessed 14 Dec 2012).

[114] Project on Ethnic Relations, *Albanians and Their Neighbors: Is the Status Quo Acceptable?*, 35-37.

[115] Xhudo, *Diplomacy and Crisis Management in the Balkans: A US foreign Policy Perspective*, 115

[116] The Globe and Mail, "The Perils of Ethnic Nationalism", 30 August, 1993, http://www.lexisnexis.com.ezproxy.usawcpubs.org/hottopics/lnacademic/ (accessed 13 Oct 2012).